bam + mac
b o o k s

ISBN-10: 0-692-65823-8
ISBN-13: 978-0-692-65823-9

Designed by Kelsey Plantas, kelseyplantas.com
Author photo by Tricia Messeroux, tmezz@bigeyephotography.com
Cover photograph, Getty Images
Edited by C.E. Williams

Visit us on the web: leilanibrown.com | fromcampustocubicle.com

DEDICATED TO MY HEARTBEAT, THE MOST IMPORTANT.

INTRODUCTION

If you are reading this book(let), chances are you have recently graduated, landed your first professional role, or at least you are preparing to do so. Congratulations and good for you!

You are our workforce's newest talent, unquestionably bright, determined and full of promise. Perhaps you have aspirations to move ahead, and this is indeed possible. That is, if you avoid some of the pitfalls that can derail a promising start.

How I wish I had someone pull me aside when I was first starting out! Luckily, the hiring committee looked past the ill-fitting suit I borrowed for the interview, and disregarded my answer about my career aspirations (which, at the time, were to quit working shortly thereafter and attend law school full-time). I got the job — in spite of myself — and so far, with mentorship, sponsorship, and learning from my mistakes, I have had a pretty rewarding experience.

Over the course of my career, I have had the occasion to network, mentor, and speak to hundreds of young professionals, offering my tips on surviving and thriving in the workplace. A few years ago, I picked the top 25 *(yes, there are a few more of these tips)*, started sharing that list, and, to my surprise, it started circulating. Soon, this book(let) was born.

3 QUICK NOTES BEFORE WE BEGIN:

1. Why do I call this a book(let)?
   It is more than a pamphlet, quite
   a bit less than a book. But, most
   importantly, I hope that it is a quick,
   easy and fun read – something to
   peruse over breakfast, during a
   subway commute, or in the waiting
   room at the doctor's office.

2. This is designed for young
   professionals, just getting started
   on their career journeys. But, if you
   know a few "experienced" colleagues
   who might benefit from the tips,
   simply rip out the introduction that
   identifies the target reader and
   discreetly slip it under their keyboard
   when they go to lunch.

3. Yes, I am a woman. But, this is not an advice book for women. This has been developed for young professionals of all backgrounds. (For example, the advice about shoes fully applies to gentlemen as well!)

Let's keep the dialogue going. Join a continued discussion about the tips, career journeys and the workplace on Twitter, Instagram, LinkedIn, Facebook (and any other social media) using the hashtag **#fromcampustocubicle.**

I would love to hear from you.

Good Luck,

Leilani

Visit us at: leilanibrown.com | fromcampustocubicle.com
Twitter @leilanimarkets | Instagram: LeilaniMarkets
Facebook.com/leilanimarkets

THE TIPS

1. Work Hard and Deliver Results.

2. Learn the Business.

3. Always Be Curious.

4. Develop Your Own Personal Brand.

5. Avoid Taking Photos With Cocktails.

6. Maintain Your Integrity.

7. Dress for Success.

8. Buy Good Shoes and Maintain Them.

9. Write Well.

10. Admit What You Don't Know.

11. Pause.

12. It's Not All About You.

13. When You Fail, Learn.

14. Pay Yourself First.

15. Avoid Gossip.

16. Use Social Media Wisely.

17. Own the Mistakes.

18. Relationships Matter.

19. Do Not Steal.

20. Don't Be a Jerk.

21. Work Parties Are Still Work.

22. Feedback is a Gift.

23. Be Yourself.

24. Hoot with the Owls & Soar with the Eagles.

25. Be Enthusiastic.

WORK HARD & DELIVER RESULTS.

1

We will start with the most obvious
tip because it is one worth repeating...
work hard and deliver results.
During the first few years of your
career, your job is to learn as much
as possible and make your boss' job
easier. Quite simply, you are there
to deliver. With enthusiasm. Without
error. And on time. So just do it.

LEARN THE BUSINESS.

2

Irrespective of your specific role, you should make a point of learning about the company and the industry in which you work. This is the time to ask questions, look for opportunities to join meetings, and to volunteer for extra projects. Make every effort to understand your company fully, how it generates revenue and profit, and how your role contributes value to the organization.

3

ALWAYS BE
CURIOUS.

It has never been easier to explore new ideas, cultures, and emerging technologies. In addition to learning your industry, you should explore what interests you and keep up with our dynamic and changing world.

- Read, skim, or watch the news daily. This should include <u>all</u> news (business, politics, sports, and pop culture — all are potentially interesting in a "water cooler" discussion or may even be relevant to your role.)

- Occasionally read something with which you disagree or watch the news broadcast from another country — an outside-in view can challenge or refine your thinking.

- Attend or participate in a free learning event in your community, online or after-hours...

**School may be over,
but your education is not.**

4

DEVELOP YOUR OWN PERSONAL BRAND.

Who are you?
What do you do?
What makes you stand out from the rest?

All professionals, especially those with longevity, have developed and cultivated positive personal brands and reputations. Through your actions, your work and your own personal narrative, make a declarative statement about who you are.

Be known for something — hopefully, something good.

5

**AVOID TAKING PHOTOS
WITH COCKTAILS.**

This is just a good thing to learn and practice early. Photos such as these generally look bad, can be taken out of context and may create an image you don't want to have to defend later on.

So, before you smile for the camera, put the glass down.

MAINTAIN YOUR INTEGRITY.

Integrity matters.

Having a set of personal values,
and adhering to them, even in the
most challenging of circumstances,
is important.

Keep your promises and be honest.

7

DRESS FOR SUCCESS.

"People will stare,
make it worth their while."

- Harry Winston

You don't have to break the bank to be well dressed and have a great personal appearance. And, believe it or not, you can even have a little bit of fun with fashion.

Rule 1:
Read the cues of the organization. If everyone is wearing a suit, you should do the same.

Rule 2:
Dress for the position you want.

Rule 3: Invest in good quality clothing and shoes (and wear them over and over again — it's perfectly ok).

Rule 4:
Maintain your items — it matters. Keep them clean, tailored, polished and perfect.

You should find a look and style that is appropriate, authentic and makes you feel good — that becomes your signature look.

8

BUY GOOD SHOES & MAINTAIN THEM.

And while we are on the topic
of dressing well...I thought
I would double down and
talk about one of my favorite
topics — <u>shoes</u>!

In my experience and
opinion, if your feet hurt,
life will be unnecessarily
harder. But, with the right
shoes, you can feel like
you are on solid ground,
accomplish great things
or even feel a bit special.
Once you make the
investment, find a great
shoemaker and visit
them often.

Trust me — you won't
be disappointed.

9

WRITE WELL.

there
_____

their
_____

they're
_____

In the age of email, Twitter and Facebook, we have become very casual and lazy with our written communication. Writing well - without error, with precision, clearly and concisely - will differentiate you.

It also creates opportunities for the spotlight to shine on you. When a member of my team prepares something that is perfect and ready, I will forward it "as is" so that they can receive credit. If it's not ready, I can't share it...and I don't.

ADMIT WHAT YOU DON'T KNOW.

10

Let me let you in on a secret — you were hired because of your potential. (Even executives are hired based on their potential). Your first order of business is to learn. Ask questions now. There are no stupid questions... yet. But, a year from now, if you are asking what EBITDA means, or what unit handles M&A, or who the COO is, then...that's stupid.

PAUSE.

II

If you are lucky enough to be in this world of work for enough time, somone will make you angry. Not something, but someone. So mad, in fact, that you are ready to give voice to the incredible injustice by telling them exactly what you think, that their mother dresses them funny, and that you don't believe that they are, in fact, qualified to be in the same room with you.

And you might even be right. But those things, like many others, are best left unsaid. So, the real strength comes in your ability to PAUSE.

Wait 24 hours before you respond. You will likely find that your anger has subsided, and you are able to give a far better response, if there is a need to respond at all. Because you cannot take it back.

IT'S NOT ALL ABOUT YOU.

12

 Things happen. Sometimes things happen to us. And sometimes we don't like these things. But when they do, I encourage you to take a step back and realize that there is a bigger picture. That the change you don't like, the acknowledgment you didn't get, the extra task at the last minute, was not likely directed at you. Your boss didn't wake up with a master plan to ruin your day.

Get over it.

13

WHEN YOU FAIL, ~~LRN~~ LEARN.

We all fail. If you are lucky, you will fail a lot early in your career, recover quickly and with little long-standing impact. But, when you fail or lose, don't lose the lesson. Don't miss the opportunity to ask yourself... *What could I have done differently? How will I handle that next time?*

PAY YOURSELF FIRST.

14

Chances are you are eligible to participate in your organization's 401K or 403B plan and able to take advantage of the company match. ENROLL AND MAX IT OUT! Why? You will establish early savings habits, you will benefit from compounding interest, you won't miss the cash from your paycheck, and you will take full advantage of the "free" money granted by the company match.

The sad truth is that we are not invincible. We all need to save for retirement, a home, a rainy day — these inevitabilities are closer than you think.

Fine Print: This is not investment advice.

15

AVOID GOSSIP.

IF YOU DON'T
HAVE ANYTHING
NICE TO SAY,
SIT NEXT TO ME.

Ok, let's admit it — we all snicker at a little gossip now and then.

But, here is what I learned a long time ago: it's best to operate in facts vs. hearsay, truth vs. innuendo, and official messages vs. speculation. If you avoid gossip, and you are known to avoid it, you will rarely have to defend who said what. But if you engage in it, it's a slippery slope. You might find that the same people who bring you gossip about others are sharing gossip about you to others.

USE
SOCIAL
MEDIA
WISELY.

16

Use your personal social media as if the company is watching. Because it is.

Ok, maybe the company doesn't have 24-hour surveillance on your Instagram account but what if you post photos of a wonderful night out with your friends at 3 AM but decide to call in sick with the Ebola virus at 8 AM? Or, what if you decide to pen a rant on your Facebook account about how much you dislike one of your colleagues and an online friend is her relative? Or, tweet about how excited you are about project #quickdial and sensitive information is leaked? These posts can surface easily and have a very negative impact on your career.

OWN THE MISTAKES.

My fault!

17

We all make mistakes, have stumbles, or make errors. When this happens, and it is indeed your fault, it is important to be personally accountable for those errors. Don't place blame elsewhere — simply own it, correct it and move on quickly.

Accountability will be important as you progress in your career.

18

RELATIONSHIPS MATTER.

Yes, you will see these people again.

I have been working in my industry for over 20 years. I am amazed by how many people remember me from my first years in the business. I am proud to say that many of them recall positive interactions. I have kept in touch with many of them, and have been able to call on them throughout my career and them on me. Their kids often call on me as well.

Develop meaningful and productive relationships throughout your professional career and you will not be sorry. It pays off long term.

DO NOT STEAL.

19

This may sound like one of the Ten Commandments, but, truly, let's talk about theft. Obviously, stealing money from the company is bad. But no one is going to hand you a checkbook to do that in your first week. But consider some other forms of stealing: abuse of time, falsifying your expense reports, taking home office supplies, or spending a ridiculous amount of your workday on social media. You can survive a long time getting away with these behaviors, but it sets up a lifetime of poor work habits.

20

DON'T BE
A JERK.

HELLO
MY NAME IS

Nice

Someone once shared an axiom that has stuck with me: "People do business with people they like." I know that to be true. Being abrupt, abrasive, overly-opinionated, or rude to your colleagues — and everyone in your company is a colleague, from the mailroom to boardroom because we are all in this together — will do very little. You will be avoided. You will not be granted the benefit of the doubt... ever. And when you implode — and you will — no one will help you.

WORK PARTIES ARE STILL WORK.

Soon, you are going to be invited to a meeting after hours. It will be held at a local restaurant or bar, your colleagues will be there, and food and beverages will be served. You might even hear music that entices a certain gentleman from accounting to do The Running Man.

This "meeting" is called a work party and is not to be confused with a regular party. You are still being observed, cultivating relationships with your colleagues, and you should still exhibit some level of decorum.

This doesn't mean you have to be a stick in the mud — in fact you should participate and enjoy the festivities. But, resist the urge to get your fill of the open bar or bust a move on top of the tables. Remember...this is still a work function.

22

FEEDBACK IS A GIFT.

It might surprise you, but some bosses have a hard time giving feedback. Don't assume that, if your boss hasn't shared feedback, things are going well. This is not always true. Indeed, one of the worst things is for there to be an issue, and for you to be unaware until the annual review.

You should get into the habit of soliciting feedback on a regular basis. Ask...*How am I doing?*
What feedback do you have for me?
What should I do differently?

If you receive negative or challenging feedback, simply listen, and demonstrate a willingness to learn and correct.

23

BE YOURSELF.

Be your authentic self. Don't waste any time or energy trying to be anything other than who you are. When we operate and work from a place of authenticity, we are at our strongest. That is when we do our best work.

HOOT WITH THE OWLS & SOAR WITH THE EAGLES.

24

Ah to be twenty-something again! I remember the fun and late nights of beer, wine, and Karaoke. But here is the contract you must make with yourself: if you are going to be up late hooting with the owls, then you had better be prepared to be up early and soaring with the eagles.

It's possible to enjoy yourself and keep your job!

BE
ENTHUSIASTIC.

25

Finally, **have fun**.

Go into this experience with an
open mind, an open heart and
full of enthusiasm.

Please accept my very best wishes.

GOOD LUCK!

TO THE DREAM TEAM ...

KELSEY PLANTAS, talented graphic designer for setting the art direction and illustration for this project;

TRICIA MESSEROUX, photographer extraordinaire who makes magic here and elsewhere.

AS WELL AS...

To my loving family, wonderful friends, and the many gracious colleagues with whom I have had the good fortune to work, for their encouragement, patience, support, suggestions and belly laughs while I finished this book(let)...

THANK YOU!

26

UPGRADE YOUR EMAIL.

kegmaster@college.edu

Now that you have graduated, it's time to upgrade your email address. Select a clear simple one that closely resembles your name and is, hopefully, easy to remember.

Abandon prior email addresses that are overly cute, provocative, or controversial. In addition, it's a great time to move away from your school's domain address and consolidate to one account.

Want more???...

JOIN US FOR A CONTINUED DISCUSSION

leilanibrown.com
fromcampustocubicle.com

Connect with us on:

Twitter: **@leilanimarkets**

Instagram: **@LeilaniMarkets**

Facebook: **facebook.com/leilanimarkets**

Using the hashtag **#fromcampustocubicle**

MY TIPS

_____

_____

_____

_____

_____

_____

_____

_____

_____

MY TIPS

_____

_____

_____

_____

_____

_____

_____

_____

_____

MY TIPS

_____

_____

_____

_____

_____

_____

_____

_____

MY TIPS

_____

_____

_____

_____

_____

_____

_____

_____

_____